GREAT YARMOUTH THEN & NOW

IN COLOUR

MICHAEL TEUN

BEST WISHES
MICHAEL M Teun. 2012.

First published in 2012

The History Press
The Mill, Brimscombe Port
Stroud, Gloucestershire, GL5 2QG
www.thehistorypress.co.uk

British Library Cataloguing in Publication Data.
A catalogue record for this book is available from the British Library.

ISBN 978 0 7524 8288 0

Typesetting and origination by The History Press
Printed in India.

CONTENTS

ACKNOWLEDGEMENTS

Once again I am indebted to the many people who, over the years, have kindly lent me their photographs: they made this book possible.

Thanks to the staff, both past and present, of the reference library, Great Yarmouth for their assistance. To the many people who have assisted me over the years with information, including the late George Rye with his work on the Whitefriars. I am indebted once again to Joan Lobban for correcting my bad grammar.

Finally, thanks to my dear wife Susanne: without her great patience and encouragement this book would not have materialized. This book I dedicate to her and say thank you.

ABOUT THE AUTHOR

Michael Teun is already the author of several local history books, including *Rows of Great Yarmouth, Parts 1-6*. As a young man of seventeen he worked in Broad Row, one of the most historical Rows which, over the years, he has specialised in. He soon realised how little he knew about his home town and, determined to find out more, he began his research. The hobby became a passion, and today his knowledge of the history of the borough is unsurpassed. He is currently working on several new projects connected with Great Yarmouth's Rows.

INTRODUCTION

This pictorial tour of Great Yarmouth, it is hoped, will take the reader on a journey back in time, to walk the streets so familiar to our fathers and forefathers. The present generation is growing up surrounded by modern flats and wide streets, but once Yarmouth contained Rows so narrow that people on one side could almost shake hands with people on the other side through their windows.

The passage of time has certainly erased much that reminds us of the poverty, long working hours and unemployment of bygone days, when life was hard. The flats and maisonettes built on the old Middlegate are a far cry from the overcrowding, crude sanitation and lack of amenities suffered by tenants before the Second World War. The camera has recorded many of these scenes, so we can now enjoy them without experiencing the hardship of living in that age – making us long for the days that are no more.

Looking at these photographs reminds us how much has been lost. The photographs here are arranged to travel from Row 3, at the north end, through the old streets of Great Yarmouth. The ends of the Rows that survive today will be shown, and how the modern road pattern follows the lines of the old Rows. The tour will pass many 'slums', though the townsfolk I have talked to can confirm that these so-called slums were in fact their castles. However, scrupulously clean kitchens could not disguise the fact that many walls were being held together by wallpaper; that a post in one corner was holding up the ceiling; and the dark stain that drew attention to the gaudy colours of the wallpaper was indeed a damp patch.

In former days, food would not keep for any length of time. Shopping trips were thus made almost daily, and few goods were pre-packed; there would be a long wait while each item was weighed and packed. The 1950s saw a change in shopping habits; the days of the small shop were numbered. The first self-service shop in the town was Elmo's in the Market Place, with the first national supermarket, Fine Fare, opening in 1962.

The photographers of the past left a legacy that enables us to see what our town was once like. Middlegate Street, for example, was an area scheduled for clearance prior to 1939, though the outbreak of hostilities put an end to any hope of improvements. By the end of the war, however, few of the buildings were considered to be worth preserving, and the whole district became one of several reconstruction sites in Great Yarmouth. It is with all these changes to our town in mind that this book has been compiled. I would like to invite you to join me in a tour of the ancient back streets of Great Yarmouth, with a snapshot of the town as it appears today.

BOULTER'S ROW, NORTHGATE STREET

BOULTER'S ROW, OR Row 3, looking east. The covered way at the east end can be seen. The carving fixed to the pediment belonging to a public house, namely the Kings Arms on Northgate Street, can also clearly be seen.

The Rows were mainly named after tradesmen and taverns. The Boulter family, bakers, resided at the north-eastern corner of this Row. Row 3 was a particularly wide Row, measuring 9ft across in some parts – quite the opposite of the famous Kitty Witches Row, only 27in wide. The Row at the west end opened up into Laughing Image Corner, an open area which took its name from the images of two children in niches on the front of a building on the north side. The open gutter, seen on the right of the Row, accumulated much filth, which must have helped to spread disease.

SADLY, VAST AREAS of these unique Rows were destroyed by enemy action during the last war. Along the principal roads, however, remains of the Rows can be seen. Although many are only a few yards in length, the way in which adjacent properties joined above the Row can still be seen.

The famous body-snatcher Thomas Vaughan, alias Smith, rented premises here in 1827 – not at Row 6, as noted in many histories. Vaughan's case was tried at Norwich Assizes on 11 August 1828. All the court papers, as well as the *Norwich Mercury*, mention 'Vaughan's rented premises in Boulter's Row'. The police report also states 'a search of a house in Boulter's Row was made by Peter Coble', mayor's officer of Yarmouth. Fences were later put up around St Nicholas' churchyard to prevent a repetition of the crime.

FULLER'S HILL

FULLER'S HILL, SOUTH side, in the 1890s. The hill had been lowered over the years, leaving the houses shown standing proud. The public house to the right was The Jolly Waterman on the corner of George Street.

These houses, of considerable antiquity, were all demolished by 1902. Tradition says that Fuller's Hill is where the first settlement of Great Yarmouth was made. Archaeological excavations in this area in the 1970s revealed eleventh-century occupation layers, Fuller's Hill being the highest part of the sandbank on which the town was formed. At what period the name was acquired is not known but it has existed for centuries; an ancient family called Fuller once possessed property there.

George Street, the oldest street in the town, commences from the crown of the hill and runs south. Immediately opposite, on the north side, there was a continuation of it until a junction was formed with White Horse Plain. This latter was called

Fuller's Passage. Electric trams came to Great Yarmouth in 1902 but unfortunately the system plan was drawn up with some haste. The double track over Fuller's Hill was never profitable and was soon relegated to depot journeys only (except for the occasional special). A new bridge over the River Bure opened in 1972, with a new road scheme and the resulting demolition of almost all of the picturesque range of old shops and houses on the hill.

TODAY ONLY ONE shop, Twinkles, remains, along with the Crystal public house (sadly empty). At Falcon Court, seen on the south side, the flats still stand proud, though further back from the road.

ST ANDREW'S CHURCH AND SCHOOL

ST ANDREW'S CHURCH and School was on the south-west corner of Fuller's Hill and North Quay. The first stone was laid on 30 November 1859. The contract for building was £1,050. In March 1864 a schoolroom was built adjoining the church. This cost an extra £500. The church was consecrated in 1860, with room for 400 parishioners, for the benefit of the waterside population.

Before the erection of this church, divine service was performed in a sail loft on the west side of the road. The church was built on an open space formerly known as Bessey's Piece; a family of that name owned the saw pits that are known to have occupied this site. In May 1961 St Andrew's finally closed. It was demolished three years later to make room for a garage and offices for Norfolk Motor Services.

NORTH QUAY TODAY. The car park for Staples stands on the site of St Andrew's church and School. Norfolk Motor Services, as already mentioned, took over the site in 1964. The premises were destroyed by fire in 1984 and the firm was later taken over by H.S. Neave. Comet discount warehouse opened here two years later. At the rear of the old school were the premises of E. Ward, listed in 1959 as a general merchant. As a young lad living in George Street I would go around the local houses collecting paper and rags to sell to this trader. I was a pupil at the school in the 1950s, the headmistress being Mrs Spandler and my first teacher Miss Kemp. Trains ran along North Quay. Great excitement was felt if you were in the playground when the train passed. Each train was preceded by a railway man carrying a red flag.

THE BREWERY STORES, NORTH QUAY

THE BREWERY STORES was the last building to survive at this site. It was demolished in 1997 to allow an Aldi supermarket to be built. The brewery became known as Lacons from 1760. It controlled 300 pubs, employed 150 workers and made Yarmouth a top destination for beer lovers. In 1883 the brewery site ran from Church Plain to George Street, and consisted of a large yard with an enclosed entrance. Row 14 was to the north and Row 21 to the south. In 1895 work commenced on building the new brewery stores on North Quay. A rail siding was brought into the store from the quay tramway, and four trains per week were sent to London, each carrying the company name. The building was erected upon ground formerly occupied by cottages, malting room, old tan room and the Lord Nelson public house. It extended from George Street to North Quay and from Row 13 to Row 17.

THE SITE TODAY. In 1957 Lacons came under the Whitbread umbrella, with the latter taking a stake of 20 per cent. In 1965 an offer of £3.2 million was made by Whitbread for the whole company. Brewing and bottling in the town ceased at the Church Plain site in 1968. The buildings were demolished in 1973. The North Quay stores were modified to receive bulk deliveries by road and the local public houses were served from there with Whitbread products. Lacons suffered considerable damage in the Second World War, and part of brewery stores on North Quay was destroyed in 1942. During this raid the firemen decided to rush to the brewery to save it from the ravaging flames while other buildings burnt. The stores were rebuilt in 1948, but by 1988 they were surplus to requirements, with local pubs served from distribution depots further afield.

SAYS CORNER, NORTH QUAY

THE ORIGINAL ROW 17, on the left, was demolished in 1895 to make way for Lacons' brewery stores, already mentioned. The Row later numbered 17 was in fact the original Row 18, or Says Corner South. Rows 17 and 18 extended from George Street to the east boundary of Says Corner, a 37ft opening from North Quay.

The name Says appears to derive from a Mr Sayers, a baker, who had his bakery in this Row over 100 years ago. Another baker, Mr Charles Harwood, is found in the 1905 *Kelly's Directory* at No. 5, Row 18. This building was later converted into a warehouse. In 1884 a cow-keeper resided, or had his sheds, in Row 17, and Mr Angel, a sweep, was a familiar sign with his brush in this Row.

TODAY THE SUPERMARKET Aldi is on the site of Row 17. The road follows the old line of both Row 17 and Row 18. The origin of Yarmouth Rows has been the subject of much debate, but almost any medieval town will furnish examples of narrow passages leading off the main street at frequent intervals. Typically, these passages led to separate properties, each humbler than the great houses on the main street's frontage. Yarmouth is unique: the passages to houses behind the frontages, which normally peter out into a garden, run on to join another passage (made for the same purpose) on the next street, this being the only way of building on the narrow limit between the river and the sea. Hence they came to be joined, and through passages, known as Rows, were formed.

THE CONGE

THE EAST END of the Conge, *c.* 1939. This photograph shows the buildings between Row 22 and Row 24 being demolished to extend the Conge through to the Market Place. Five cottages in Row 22 and Row 24 were purchased for the sum of £170: these too were demolished. The site of Row 22 today forms the north pavement of the Conge, which originally ran only from North Quay to George Street. Clearance of this area began on the south side, making possible a large playground for the children. Moves to clear the worst of the Rows began in 1936, but had made little progress by the outbreak of war in 1939. In the end it was German bombing raids, notably in 1941, which did much of the work, destroying or damaging beyond repair large areas of the old town.

THE EAST END of the Conge today follows the old line of Row 22 on the left and Row 24 on the right. (The gutter of No. 8 Market Place, the building to the left with three storeys, can be picked out in the earlier photograph.) The original Conge can be considered one of the most ancient parts of the town. Henry I appointed a provost or a collector of duties, who resided in the Conge. *Congee* is a French term used in relation to the clearances that ships' masters had to obtain from the authorities, after having paid all dues and demands, before departure. Hence the area was anciently called the King's Conge, and the quay adjoining the Lords' Quay. The only wide thoroughfare running east to west originally was Friars Lane, at the south end, and Fuller's Hill at the north.

NORTH QUAY

NUMBERS 36-39 North Quay. On the north side of Row 28, to the far left, stood a dairy belonging to George Todd, and the sight of cows returning from the Cobholm and Southtown marshes was commonplace. Next is the Falcon public house, formerly known as the Excursion Train. The building was rebuilt in 1895. A carved falcon, the crest of the Lacon family, was found in the bar. When the North Quay was flooded – which often happened – the beer barrels in the old cellar floated about. Mr Harwood, next door at No. 37, was a very popular hairdresser and, like most Yarmouth barbers, he always had a tale to tell. Next is Self's Garage, with its sign above. Later on,

Mr Self took over the complete site. Row 31 is found to the right of the small cottage. Watling's Malt House can just be seen on the far right.

THE OFFICE BLOCK found on the site today stands between the old lines of Row 28 to the left and a sign saying 'Row 31' to the right. Self's opened new and enlarged showrooms in 1962, taking in the ground floor of the old Falcon public house but keeping the upper storeys intact. The small cottage to the right of the garage was demolished to widen Row 31 and to enable access to the workshop to the rear of the garage. Self's, after many years of trading, closed in 1978. Soon after, the buildings were demolished to build a new office block for Frans Maas. Row 31 was named 'Nine Parish Row', for which no satisfactory explanation is known. Perhaps it may be a corruption of Non Parish Row, implying it was the responsibility of the nearby Whitefriars to maintain it?

BOULTON'S STORE, NORTH QUAY

BOULTON'S DEPARTMENT STORE, June 1943. The lamp post with painted white lines is a reminder of air-raid precautions, an age of cars with blinkers and thick curtains. James Boulton is listed as a draper in 1905, adding 'furnisher' a few years later. Mr Boulton purchased next door, No. 56, in the 1960s to add to his store. Boulton's remained a major department store in the 1970s, with carpets hanging in the showroom like tapestries. Boulton's ran what my mother always called 'Boulton's Club', a scheme allowing goods to

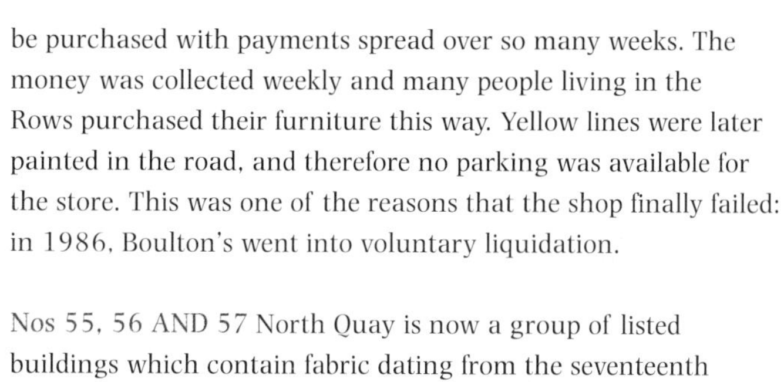

be purchased with payments spread over so many weeks. The money was collected weekly and many people living in the Rows purchased their furniture this way. Yellow lines were later painted in the road, and therefore no parking was available for the store. This was one of the reasons that the shop finally failed: in 1986, Boulton's went into voluntary liquidation.

Nos 55, 56 AND 57 North Quay is now a group of listed buildings which contain fabric dating from the seventeenth century and fragments of an older construction. In the seventeenth century records indicate that it was a merchant's house relating to the important historic commercial activity of the quay. The site in the twelfth century formed part of the already mentioned Whitefriars Friary. Numbers 55 and 56 had been vacant and neglected for twenty years and were in a state of severe deterioration. Some emergency repairs were undertaken in 2003 to prevent collapse. The repair and conversion of this group of buildings started in 2007, but the buildings proved so fragile that the contractor decided to work from the cellar upwards and to underpin the buildings. Number 56 was a school for training servant girls for many years, but later was taken in as part of the store.

No. 86 George Street

THIS PHOTOGRAPH OF No. 86 George Street was taken in 1943. The east end of Row 34 can be seen to the right. The building had iron wall-anchors with the date 1638, and the letters E.T., formed into a house mark. The use of wall anchors became widespread because of unstable soil conditions. Fine houses dating from the early seventeenth century existed in great numbers in the area. The best examples were found in the principal streets like George Street. The last of these dwellings to survive was found in Howard Street South, but sadly it was demolished in the late 1980s. To the left is the west end of Row 33. George Street began at Fuller's Hill, and ran to Hall Quay (originally called Northgate, though not to be confused with a later street named after a gate in the town wall). The name Northgate was later changed to Conge Street and finally to George Street.

PATTERSON CLOSE FOLLOWS the old line of Row 34. This image shows the rear of the buildings with the gable end. The original site of No. 86 George Street is the wall and bushes to the left. Redevelopment of this area, between George Street and the Market Place, began in the early 1950s. Blocks of flats replaced the old Row's houses. In more recent years the second-floor flats have been demolished, turning the bottom flats into town houses. Patterson Close is named after Arthur Patterson, the Yarmouth naturalist, who was born in nearby Row 36. In 1964, when excavations were being made for a new block of flats (now the west end of Patterson Close), an old mortared flint wall some 3ft thick was found. Again, was this part of the already mentioned Whitefriars Friary? Terraced houses marked '1896' survive at the west end of Row 34.

ROW 45, ST FRANCIS WAY

ROW 45 RAN from North Quay to George Street. It was known as St John's Head Row after a public house which stood at the south-west corner. In early documents – including a court case in 1312 – the name is written 'Syngen', a remarkable survival of a Row name through the centuries. These documents prove that St John's Head Row is an early thoroughfare. Today the public house still stands on the corner of St Francis Way.

The town's mortuary, at the north-west corner, opened in 1899, with the stone entrance and large wood doors being in this Row. Demolished in 1959, it was relocated to Northgate Hospital. Perhaps the most severely damaged of all the Rows, on 11 April 1941 George Street was hit by four high-explosive bombs. One fell on a public shelter near this Row, killing seven occupants.

WORK COMMENCED WITH the construction of St Francis Way on the south side in 1952. A quantity of human bones from the burial ground of the Whitefriars was disturbed by a mechanical excavator on the north side of the road. An error on the Ordnance Survey map of 1883 puts the 'site of Franciscan Priory' to the north of the Broad Row. Actually, St Francis was the saint of the Greyfriars in Middlegate Street. Nobody seems to have picked up this error, however, and so the council thought it fit and proper to name the newly constructed road St Francis Way.

The block of buildings facing North Quay, which protrude somewhat from the building line, may indicate the old property boundary of the Whitefriars: Row 31 to the north, George Street to the east and Row 45 to the south.

BROAD ROW

BROAD ROW, LOOKING towards George Street, in the early 1980s. Just visible on the left is Plattens' food mini-market, which opened in 1966. These premises were formerly owned by Mr Wright, a baker. In the 1950s Mr Mead opened his restaurant next door at No. 22. Charles Allen's music shop, whose sign is clearly visible, was at No. 23. Charles Allen and his wife moved from Wales and set up a shop in Northgate Street. Trade was quite brisk and they soon moved to larger premises in the Broad Row. Charles was joined by his son John and the business expanded. They moved premises to the upper section of the Market Gates complex,

able to succeed where other businesses had failed. They are now located on the lower level of Market Gates, opposite the bus station.

THE FIRST MENTION of the Yarmouth Rows came in 1286, when the number in each leet (ward) was given. From this we find a total of some 140. The original Broad Row was formerly known as 'Kingston House Row'. The first mention was in the session roll of 1295, when the daughter of Thomas le Meiser was convicted of a burglary in the house of John Allen, who was a bailiff. 'Broad Row' was almost certainly one of the Rows mentioned in the 1286 document. Palmer in his *Perlustration* named many well-to-do Yarmouth families who lived in the Broad Row. The deeds for premises in this Row support this. With all the fine buildings here the Row had to be wide, to give room for frontage.

HALL QUAY

HALL QUAY, SOME 250 yards in length, is an open area. Before the Town Hall opened, it was known as 'the Foreland'. In this image, the post office can clearly be seen. This establishment moved to Hall Quay in 1840 from Row 63. The first post office was established in Row 107 in the seventeenth century, and the building was thereafter known as the Post House. In 1870, the Hall Quay post office moved to the old Corn Hall, Regent Street. The building originally had a cut-flint frontage similar to that of the Duke's Head, which it adjoins. Note the stagecoach outside the Duke's Head. It was from this inn that the London coach set out. On the front of the building a tablet bears the date 1609 and the initials R.I.S. The house would then have been even larger than it is today, for much of it was demolished in 1901 when restoration work was carried out.

HALL QUAY BECAME one of the most fashionable parts of the town. In the sixteenth and seventeenth centuries, when the wealth and prosperity of Yarmouth must have been the envy of many large towns, a number of its merchants built fine houses. Several had elegant fronts of cut and squared flint and the Duke's Head is a splendid example of that period. Anyone looking at a plan of the town must wonder why the South Quay building line did not join up with North Quay. Perhaps this gap was waterlogged and easily flooded at some period? Note that the shop front on the corner of Hall Quay and George Street, to the left, is shown on the 1860 photograph as a private house.

NOS 15-19 HALL QUAY

HALL QUAY, *c.* 1876. Building work is here in progress to rebuild John Clowes' grocery shop. In 1845 Clowes purchased the business from the Morgan family, who had been trading as grocers since 1787 on this site. The building to the left was a draper's shop belonging to William Hunter. After the rebuilding work, John Clowes also purchased this shop. The tall, bay-fronted building at that time was the residence of Lady Orde, and on the right-hand side of that building we find the end of Row 57. Next along the quay is the Star and Garter public house on the south-west corner of this Row; today, the Star and Garter is on the other side of the Row. This public house was demolished, along with Lady Orde's house, and was rebuilt on the other side of the Row when the bank next door, Lacon Youell, wished to expand.

HALL QUAY FROM Haven Bridge. Lloyds Bank, to the right, absorbed the old Lacon Youell bank in 1918. Today seven windows can be seen, but in 1870s photograph only five are present. The later rebuild of the Star and Garter, on the site of Lady Orde's house, is seen here, with Row 57 to the right. Aldreds, with its modern brick front, was constructed after the work had been completed. The upper storeys in William Hunter's shop have not changed. Barclays bank is to the far left; the ground floor was converted into a bank in 1794. Dawson Turner was a partner and occupied the whole of the upper part of the house. In 1896 the bank amalgamated with nineteen other private banks to form Barclays.

HALL QUAY, LOOKING TOWARDS THE TOWN HALL

HALL QUAY, 1910. A tram is making its way across Hall Quay to Vauxhall Station. Clowes' Stores, already mentioned, was a long-established Yarmouth business and it had everything a grocer's shop should have – with all the delicious smells associated with them. It was stocked with candles, sugar in blue bags and butter patted into half pounds; counterweight scales with their brass weights; an old till where the prices came up on rollers. Clowes had other branches,

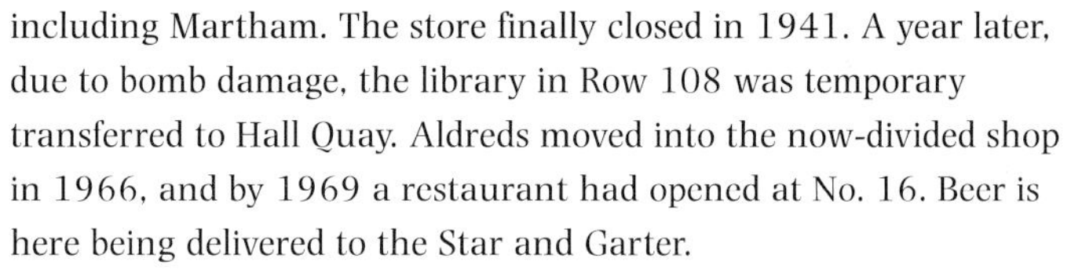

including Martham. The store finally closed in 1941. A year later, due to bomb damage, the library in Row 108 was temporary transferred to Hall Quay. Aldreds moved into the now-divided shop in 1966, and by 1969 a restaurant had opened at No. 16. Beer is here being delivered to the Star and Garter.

IN THE FIRST half of the nineteenth century, Hall Quay was known as Short Quay. The trams are long gone: the last No. 6 ran from the Market Place to the depot on 15 December 1933. With the construction of the present Haven Bridge, a new Hall Quay layout was begun in 1930, including traffic islands and gardens. This was followed in 1934 by an experimental wooden roundabout at the foot of the bridge. In 1967 the roundabout on Hall Quay was removed, to be replaced with a new traffic light system. The ornate Victorian gables found on the old Clowes' premises, No. 16, are still seen today to the left. Aldreds, with the modern brick front, astonishingly won an award at one time for its design. The Star and Garter public house is followed by Lloyds Bank. Researchers beware – the numbering of Hall Quay changed just after 1900.

HOWARD STREET SOUTH

HOWARD STREET SOUTH, looking towards Regent Street, *c.* 1925. Locals gave this part of Howard Street the name 'Blind Howard Street' because it came to an abrupt end at Row 90. In the background the gentlemen are looking up Row 74, where demolition work is in progress to make way for the arcade. The west end of Row 78 can clearly be seen. Mrs Daynes' grocer shop was to the left of Row 78; Mrs Ruth Taylor, who in 1923 was listed simply as a shopkeeper, was on the other side of the Row. Just seen in the far background is the west end of Row 73. The south side of this Row was also demolished to make way for the arcade. In 1804 the Rows were officially numbered: these numbers were painted at the end of each, as can be seen in the photograph.

THE WEST END of Row 78 is clearly visible to the right, but sadly the number has been covered with red paint. The old line of Row 74 is a small passageway leading to the arcade.

The medieval town plan was based on three main streets that ran in a north-south direction. Howard Street, one of the oldest, ran from Church Plain southwards, finishing in a dead end at Row 90. The northern end in the late eighteenth century was renamed Charlotte Street after the daughter of George IV. In 1882 the southern end was renamed Howard Street. Today it is known as Howard Street North and South, the division still being at the Broad Row.

78

ROW 74

A FAMILY LOOK out of their doors as an unknown photographer takes this picture in the early twentieth century. Note the lamp: gas lamps began to appear in many Rows in the nineteenth century, although during the hours of darkness most Rows were still formidable places for strangers. Most of the Rows were paved with pebbles from the beach: this certainly was a decided improvement on the gravel, but made walking along the Rows anything but a pleasure. Flagstones or bricks were later introduced down the centre of the Rows. A start was made in 1884 on concreting these footpaths. At one time many accidents were caused in the Rows by the unexpected opening of a door in the dark. In 1618 the authorities insisted that all doors which opened outwards must be altered.

THE VICTORIA ARCADE, then called the Central Arcade, opened in 1926. Negotiations with the many different property owners were begun by the development company, Yarmouth Central Building Estates Ltd, in 1901 and took more than twenty years to complete. Demolition and rebuilding began in 1925 and the arcade was completed some time after the General Strike in May 1926. During the Second World War, two thirds of the shops remained open in spite of the terror of intermittent bombing – although evacuation caused the population to drop to 20,000. In 1927 Aldreds' Jewellers, Eve Brown's, a costumier, Doughty's Sports Outfitters, Pike Tobacconist and Freeman, Hardy and Willis, bootmakers, were some of the well-known traders found in the arcade. In 1945 there were no shops to let; in fact, the local agent had a waiting list. The arcade was refurbished in 1987, at a cost of £400,000, and renamed.

KING STREET

KING STREET FROM Regent Road, *c.* 1927. Freeman, Hardy and Willis' shop can be seen. There had been a shoe shop on this site for over 120 years. Pocock Brothers, trading here at the turn of the century, advertised 'the walk easy special line for gentlemen' on a large painted sign on the front of the shop. The business was taken over by Freeman, Hardy and Willis in 1910. Shoe Express, the last shoe shop on this corner, closed a few years ago. Next was Hepworth's. Joseph Hepworth, a Yorkshire-born tailor, founded the business in 1864 in Leeds, and by 1890 had opened a branch at 29 Market Place. Next was David Greig's grocery shop. Most towns had their share of chain grocers: Maypole, Home and Colonial, International, Star.

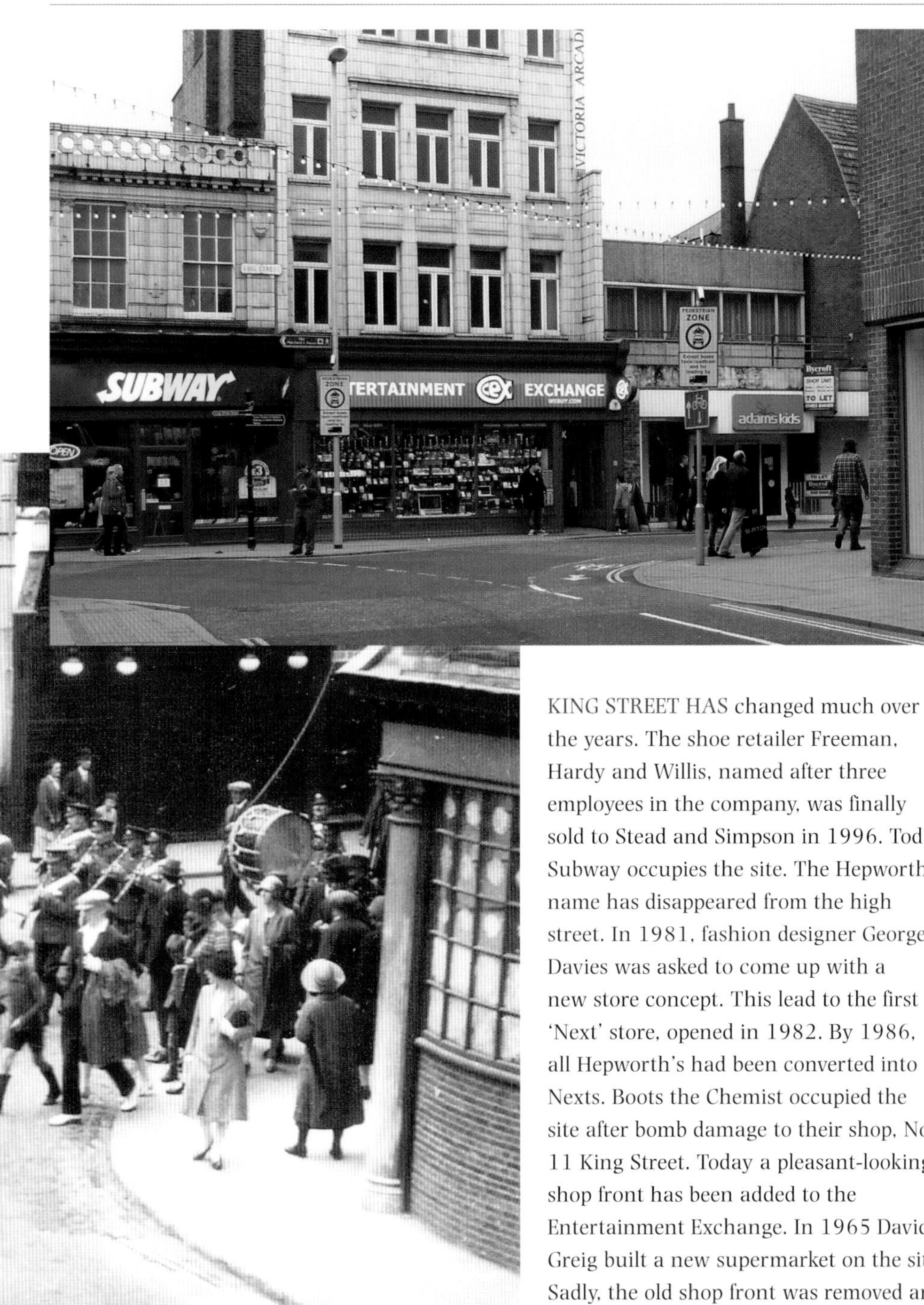

KING STREET HAS changed much over the years. The shoe retailer Freeman, Hardy and Willis, named after three employees in the company, was finally sold to Stead and Simpson in 1996. Today Subway occupies the site. The Hepworth name has disappeared from the high street. In 1981, fashion designer George Davies was asked to come up with a new store concept. This lead to the first 'Next' store, opened in 1982. By 1986, all Hepworth's had been converted into Nexts. Boots the Chemist occupied the site after bomb damage to their shop, No. 11 King Street. Today a pleasant-looking shop front has been added to the Entertainment Exchange. In 1965 David Greig built a new supermarket on the site. Sadly, the old shop front was removed and the ugly building that stands empty today was built. David Greig's was sold to Key Markets in 1972.

KING STREET LOOKING TOWARDS MARKET PLACE

ARNOLDS' DEPARTMENT STORE, on the left, was on the corner of King Street and Regent Street. It was established in 1869 by Frank and William Arnold. It was rebuilt in 1922 after a fire destroyed the premises in 1919, together with several other small shops in Regent Street. Shoppers in the 1920s had the choice of Arnolds' or Bonings' large store opposite. Opened at 5 King Street in 1860, by the 1920s the business had expanded with the purchase of adjacent shops. The rival store for Arnolds' is clearly seen – it is the bay windows on the right. In 1932 the main part of the rebuilt

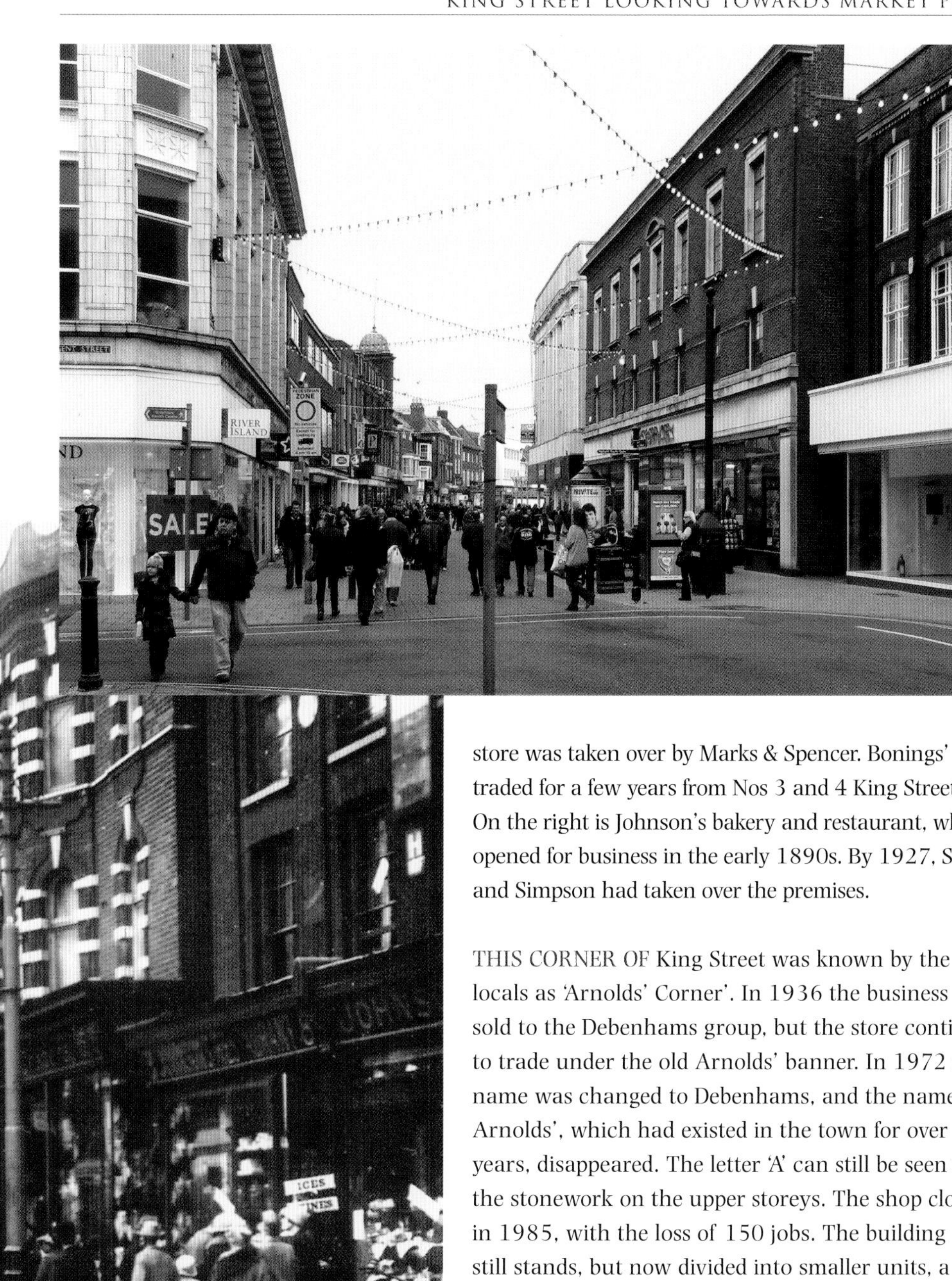

store was taken over by Marks & Spencer. Bonings' still traded for a few years from Nos 3 and 4 King Street. On the right is Johnson's bakery and restaurant, which opened for business in the early 1890s. By 1927, Stead and Simpson had taken over the premises.

THIS CORNER OF King Street was known by the locals as 'Arnolds' Corner'. In 1936 the business was sold to the Debenhams group, but the store continued to trade under the old Arnolds' banner. In 1972 the name was changed to Debenhams, and the name Arnolds', which had existed in the town for over 100 years, disappeared. The letter 'A' can still be seen in the stonework on the upper storeys. The shop closed in 1985, with the loss of 150 jobs. The building still stands, but now divided into smaller units, a reminder of days past.

Debenhams returned to the town in 2008, opening a new store in the Market Gates. Johnson's old shop is sadly one of many empty shops in the town. Marks & Spencer's store was rebuilt after the last war and moved from temporary premises into the present building in 1952.

KING STREET, LOOKING TOWARDS TOM GREEN'S CORNER

KING STREET, *c.* 1925. Stead and Simpson's shoe shop is clearly seen trading from Nos 8-10. By 1927 this large store was refitted, and the south end divided. In the 1930s Spalls opened a fancy goods shop at No. 10. Standing on the site of The Rose Tavern public house, which

closed in 1906, we next see Boots the Chemist, which moved from Regent Street in 1908 to the large rebuilt new store. This fine building extended through to Theatre Plain. Sadly, however, it was destroyed by bombs in 1941.

By the late 1950s the premises had been rebuilt again. It was divided between Samuel's the jewellers and Brighter Homes' wallpaper shop. To the far right is the Old Gallon Pot public house, always known locally as Divers.

KING STREET, LOOKING south. The building line has moved back, giving a clear view of what locals called 'Tom Green's Corner'. Tom traded here from 1900 until 1988. The corner of Regent Road today is now occupied by Greenwood's. Stead and Simpson's store, as already mentioned, was divided in the late 1920s; the old shop was rebuilt with a new front. Boots moved opposite, next to the arcade, and traded there until moving to the Market Gates. Samuel's rebuilt store is next: in recent years this was refitted, taking in the adjoining shop. Divers closed in 1974 and was demolished a few years later, to be replaced by the shops trading today – one of which buildings, sadly, is empty.

MARKET PLACE FROM KING STREET

THE MARKET PLACE, looking towards Palmer's store, from Burton's Corner. Timothy Whites' hardware shop was taken over by Boots; the shop became a gas showrooms in 1984. Palmer's menswear shop is next, separated from the main department store by the Red House public house. A model railway, built by the landlord, Mr Moore, in 1939, could be seen inside. The train could be worked by any member of the public by the insertion of a coin in a slot. Palmer's department store has dominated the Market Place for 175 years. Garwood Palmer opened his first shop at 39 Market Place in 1837. In this image, from the late 1950s, their delivery van is loading. A bus waits outside the main store.

MARKET PLACE TODAY has sadly lost some of its picturesque roof lines. Palmer's shop and the Red House (which also had became part of Palmer's), a gift shop by 1961, had all been demolished by 1966 to make way for Downs, a new supermarket. In 1975 it became Downsway and then Fine Fare, who finally closed in 1979. Today M & Co., a department store, occupies the site. Timothy Whites' became the gas showrooms, closing in 1994 to become Nationwide, seen to the left. Palmer's department store has a fine tower that looks over the Market Place: this was built in 1910, along with the bay window to the left. In 1892 the complete store was almost destroyed by a fire. However, it was rebuilt, with the addition of the further three bay widows seen today. In 1986 the store was refitted with the present shop front.

WEST SIDE OF THE MARKET PLACE

THIS PHOTOGRAPH SHOWS the west side of the Market Place on a busy summer's day in 1900. Arthur Pash's shoe shop was called Eagle Stores. Following on from Hepworth's clothiers, opened in 1890, we find the tall building of Back's wine merchants, opened in 1878. This building has not changed much to the present day. The Angel – landlord Joseph Steel, as can be seen near the roofline – was one of the oldest inns in the town. Note the window cleaner on the ledge.

The next shop, with the bay window, was a tobacconist's, run by Ernest Carpenter. Mr Palmer's eating rooms (with the sign above the shop) is followed by the Liberal Club, which opened in 1892. The Central Cinema, later called The Plaza, opened here in 1915. Further on, Cash and Co., bootmakers, and Leach's are both visible. Lacons' chimney towers over the buildings.

THE MARKET PLACE is today pedestriansed. Hepworth's opened a new store, with the Venture Restaurant trading upstairs, when the corner of Market Row was rebuilt in 1964. Today, Santander occupies the site. Back's old shop is now Clinton Cards, with 'Back to Backs' public house to the rear. The Angel lost its licence in 1939, and throughout the war years was used as a British restaurant. It was finally demolished in 1957, making way for a bookshop called The Works and the Norwich and Peterborough Building Society. Mr Carpenter's tobacconist's is at present a British Heart Foundation store. The Plaza Cinema was demolished in 1959 and Woolworths moved from Regent Road to the newly built store. That institution closed in 2009, and the building is now a Poundland store.

SOUTH END OF THE MARKET PLACE

THE SOUTH END of the Market Place, late 1920s. The Two-Necked Swan public house is to the right. Kerrison the bootmaker is trading next door. These premises became part of the Two-Necked Swan after the Second World War. The Two-Necked Swan, which, in the seventeenth century, was named 'The Three Flower De Luces', exhibited a live crocodile in a commodious room in 1806. Price of admission was 1*s*.

Mr Barnes, a well-known Yarmouth grocer, opened for business at No. 8 in 1888 and traded here until 1970. This had been the site of a grocer's shop for over 120 years. Robert Bumpsted retired in 1885, and a Mr Nichols carried on Bumpstead's business for a few years. Curry's cycle shop, at No. 9, and Frank Edwards' bakers (covered by the tree) were both demolished in 1939 to make way for road building. The Conge was taken through to the Market Place. Foulsham's Dining Rooms can just be seen through the trees. The spirit stores were licensed as the Blue Anchor.

THIS CORNER OF the Market Place is much altered, with the straight lines of modern architecture apparent. The southern pavement of the Conge was the old line of Row 24. Foulsham's Dining Rooms on the corner was bought by Lacons in 1894. Following the closure of the dining rooms, The Blue Anchor remained until 1964. It too was then demolished, and today NatWest stands on this corner. This area is now a very busy thoroughfare. Barnes' grocery shop is now Henry's. Sadly, the once fine public house the Two-Necked Swan now stands empty.

1 & 2 MARKET PLACE

BURROUGHS' STORES STOOD on the corner of the Market Place and Church Plain, the latter known by locals as 'Brewery Plain', Lacons' brewery being nearby. Number 1, with the bottles in the window, housed John Blyth, bootmaker, in the 1840s, and by 1856 Youell, a florist, was the first nurseryman to open here. He was taken over by Isaac Brunning in 1868. Number 2 was first licensed in 1772 by Richard Brighten, a brewer, but the premises seem to have been used by the family as a marriage settlement in 1741. The Burroughs family purchased the property

BURROUGHS' STORES, 1 & 2 MARKET PLACE, GT. YARMOUTH.
THE OLDEST LICENSED HOUSE IN THE DISTRICT.

in 1812 (hence the name), and traded as wine merchants for many years. Business was good and by 1878 next door had been purchased with a new shop front, as shown in the photograph. Lacons purchased the business in 1897.

BURROUGHS' WINE STORES was destroyed by an air raid on 7 May 1943. Several enemy aircraft flew very low over the town; several places were hit, including in the Lichfield, Cobholm and Regent Road areas. Burroughs' was destroyed by a direct hit. In total, over 100 houses were seriously damaged, thirteen people were killed and fifty-one injured. The George and Dragon public house on Church Plain became temporary premises for Burroughs' wine business. My late mother used to purchase bottles of Guinness here. The site stood empty until 1959, when the present Gallon Pot was built on the site. Note the pot on the top of the pole standing outside, this almost being on the site of the lamp post in the old photograph.

EAST SIDE OF THE MARKET PLACE

CELEBRATIONS IN THE Market Place to mark the Golden Jubilee of Queen Victoria in 1887. To the far left, the building with the columns was the Cambridge Dining Rooms, a favourite eating place for the market traders. The old Hospital School, with the trees in front, stands between the

dining rooms and Joseph Camps' double-fronted shop. Mr Camps was a dairyman. Robert Bell, one of the many butchers' shops on this side of the Market Place, opened next door in 1871. A barber's pole is clearly seen on the front of Edward Fulcher's, a well-known hairdresser of that time. Southey, who was listed as a 'saddler', is to the far right, with the 'God Save The Queen' sign on the front of the shop. In the far background, looking over the buildings, is the Methodist Temple on Priory Plain. Unfortunately, this has now been demolished and replaced by a roadway.

THE EAST SIDE of the Market Place has changed much over the years, with the wonderful old roof lines disappearing. The old Hospital School built in 1842, which was set back and had extensive gardens in front, was demolished and rebuilt in 1931. The new school, costing £24,142, opened in 1932; the boys worked in the northern half and the girls in the southern. Signs above the entrances can still be seen. The buildings today, those of St Nicholas Priory Middle School, are relatively recent, but infinitely better than everything more recently erected on this side of the Market Place. The now empty Co-op store to the left opened in 1935. It was thereafter known as Co-operative House. Southey's, Fulcher's, Bell's and Camps' were all demolished to build the store. The Cambridge Dining rooms have also long gone, but we still have some trees in front of the school.

FLESH SHAMBLES

A VIEW OF Queen Victoria's Diamond Jubilee in 1897. Crowds have turned out, hanging out of the windows and sitting on top of the canopies in front of the shops. This side of the market was traditionally where all the meat was sold. These 'flesh shambles' are first recorded in 1551, when all the town's butchers were required to sell their meat here. In this photograph, three butcher shops are visible: W. & R. Fletcher at No. 59; William Swann, to the right; and next door to him is Henry Barnes, all well-known local butchers. It appears all the families have come out in their finest clothes for the celebrations. Tea and coffee was available at Thompson's Dining

Rooms. Mr Forder, as shown on his sign, was a decorator. His shop looks very smart with the flag flying from his upstairs window and shields fixed to the front of the shop.

THE MARKET PLACE has seen many changes over the years. The Co-op took in many shops on the east side when it opened, including Mr Fletcher's old butcher's shop and the decorator Mr Forder's shop. Thompson's dining rooms today is the empty shop next to the Co-op. Most of the old butchers' shops had evidently changed to wholesale fruiterers by the 1950s, namely McCarthy's and Savory's.

The tall building with the bay windows was rebuilt in the 1970s. Now a café, it was for many years a dress shop and before that the site for Mr Swann's butcher shop. A Tesco opened in 1964, with the square building seen today. The entire row of fine buildings on this side has been destroyed. Tesco moved from the Market Place in 1980. This is a Spar and an Argos at present.

CORNER OF MARKET PLACE AND MARKET GATES

THIS IMAGE SHOWS Arthur Hollis's shop, which stands empty in 1973 awaiting demolition. In 1908 Arthur Hollis returned to Yarmouth from London to set up a corn business at 53 Market Place, these being temporary premises, before moving to this corner in 1910 after the purchase of the old Bull Inn. In 1970 the business expanded with the opening of a discount supermarket at the old Drill Hall on Southtown Road, and a year later another opened in the new precinct in Gorleston High Street.

In 1973 the Arthur Hollis chain was taken over by Keymarkets. Strickland's newsagents opened a new shop in these premises, replacing their two smaller shops. Note the 'Green Shield Stamp' sign between the windows. These stamps were popular: one stamp was issued for each 6*d* spent, and so large numbers of stamps had to be stuck into books to claim merchandise.

THE REBUILT SHOP is now divided into two, with a square front to match Argos together with a pleasant-looking gable end to match the adjoining buildings in Market Gates. Sentiments, a gift and card shop, is on the corner, with Western Union next door. To the left is Argos. As sales of Green Shield Stamps slowed down and retailers abandoned the scheme, the Green Shield Stamp catalogue shops were rebranded Argos in 1973. The company suspended sales of stamps in 1983; they had a short revival in 1987, but finally ceased in 1991. Tesco founder Jack Cohen, who had opened a store on the Argos site in 1964, was an advocate of trading stamps. He signed up in 1963, shortly after his competitor Fine Fare adopted stamps. Tesco became one of Green Shields' largest clients. A decision was made to finally abandon stamps in 1977.

THE FEATHERS, MARKET GATES

THE FEATHERS INN, situated in Market Gates, is probably the oldest public house in the town. In common with other tradesmen, inns, taverns and alehouses advertised their business with a sign hanging outside. A pole above the door would be garlanded with foliage, as can be seen in the photograph showing the Prince of Wales' feathers, three ostrich feathers, and the motto *Ich Dien* (which means 'I serve'). This was one of the principal inns in the town, and in 1581 was enlarged

– possibly to include the building to the right of the entrance, which (in later years) was the 'Market Room', popular on market days with country traders who stabled their horses at the Feathers. The court of Charles II were said to have been entertained here in 1672. *Norfolk Drollery*, published in 1673, has this to say about the visit: 'Soldiers and servants came down, and at the Feathers, *gratis*, got high flown'.

THE FEATHERS TODAY. Sadly, the Market Room has been demolished. The rear of the Argos store dominates the skyline. A sign with the Prince of Wales' feathers can still be seen. The Feathers was said to be the last house at which the ancient sport of 'cocking' was held. It was the custom in Norfolk for a local farmer to provide a couple of fighting cocks. Before the days of music licences, the larger public houses utilized a large room, like the demolished Market Room, for entertainment. The modern pub in some ways is both more liberal and more restricted: laws introduced in 2003 allow public houses to specify their own opening times, but in 2007 a full smoking ban was introduced. Local breweries have been absorbed by large national companies, and today public houses change hands frequently. Sadly, many have closed.

NICHOL'S AND THE ABC CINEMA

THIS IS A view of the south end of the Market Place, looking towards Theatre Plain, in the late 1960s. Nichol's Restaurant, noted for its fish and chip meals, is to the left. Note the prices: large steak and kidney pudding, 4*s*. As a young child, eating out meant a fish and chip supper, often in this restaurant. Chips from Nichol's or Kelly's stall opposite on the Market Place were a treat some days, on the way home from school. Nichol's closed in 1973 and the Market Gates shopping centre was built on the site. Trustee Bank, visible on the right, was rebuilt in 1939. The bank moved here from what was later named 'Selborne House' in Howard Street in 1859. Looking into Theatre Plain, the rear of the ABC Cinema is clearly visible.

THE MARKET PLACE today is pedestrianised, and this once-busy junction is now a place to sit and eat the famous 'Yarmouth Market Chips'. Dorothy Perkins and Boots are now on the site of Nichol's Restaurant, being part of the Market Gates Shopping Precinct. Construction work commenced in 1973. In 1974 the Conservative Club in Theatre Plain was demolished, along with the Electric House in Regent Road. A multi-storey car park opened a year later. Sainsbury's followed in 1975, but moved to St Nicholas Trading Estate in 1989. Towards the southern end of the Market Place, a covered section was built to accommodate the six-day market stalls. This, with the pedestrianisation scheme, was officially opened in 1995. The bank has changed little. The ABC – formerly 'The Regal' – just visible in the 1960s photograph was demolished in 1989.

FISH STREET

FISH STREET, WHICH leads from Theatre Plain to the Market Gates. The name comes from the market that once stood on the south side of Market Gates. In 1625 the open stalls were roofed over, and it was forbidden to sell fish anywhere else. Later, in 1844, a new market was formed, surrounded by iron balustrades. This can be seen on early photographs of the Market Place. When the Fish Wharf opened in 1869, however, this was demolished and the west end of Market Gates Road was then widened. Next to the fish market was a public house named The Jolly Butcher, later changed to Fish Stall House. The sign is clearly seen outside the Gospel Hall (or Brethren Assembly Hall, as it was listed in the 1960s). As a very young child I went to Sunday school here with my sister, being bribed with sweets to go.

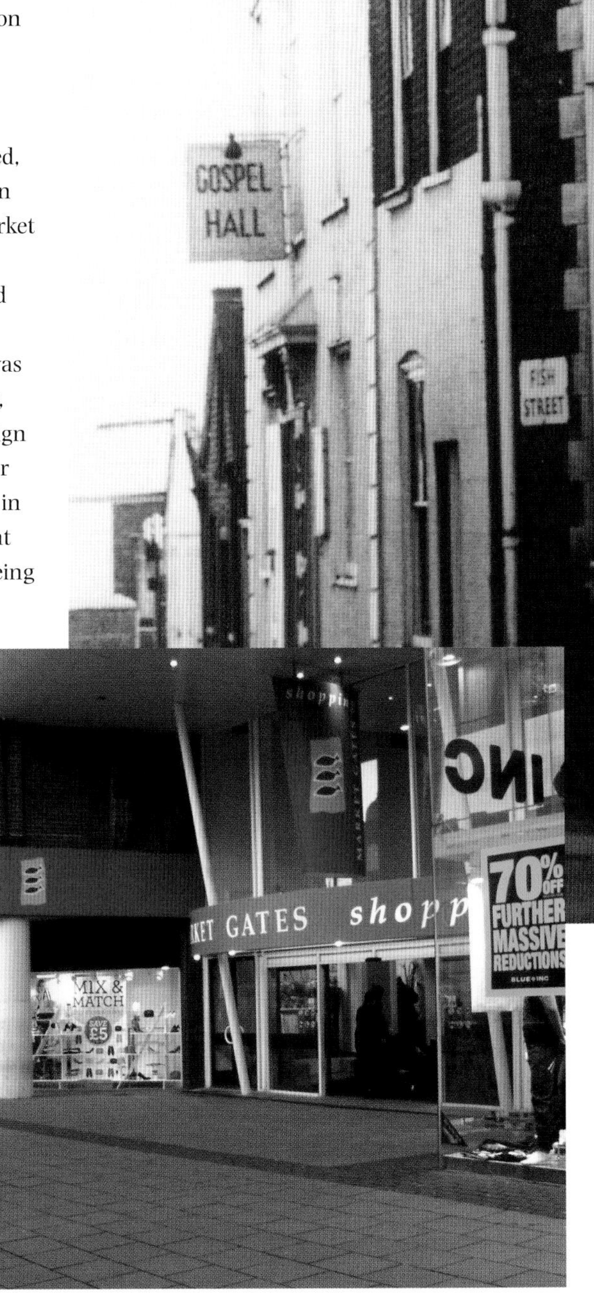

FISH STREET DISAPPEARED in 1973 with the building of the Market Gates Precinct. The site now runs though Boots from Theatre Plain. Just back from the main entrance today would have been the site of Botwright's Hairdresser, shown in the 1960s photograph. I had my hair cut there. There were to be thirty-nine shops, three supermarkets and 665 car parking spaces when the Market Gates Shopping Mall was first planned. The idea was all well and good, but we lost many landmark buildings to build it. Theatre Plain was also the main bus terminus. Opening of the Market Relief Road in 1982 joined Fuller's Hill with the new road, Temple Road, cutting through the Market Gates to join Alexandra Road. A new bus terminus was then made under the Market Gates.

THE THEATRE ROYAL, REGENT ROAD

THIS IMAGE SHOWS the Theatre Royal in around 1930. The theatre opened in 1778. The building was erected in eight months, at a cost of £1,500. The main entrance was at the northern end, facing Theatre Plain. The early years saw many full houses, but by the 1840s many small theatres were in decline. In 1849 the theatre had to close after a disastrous season. Drama productions led to a revival in the 1870s with pantomimes and plays. By the 1890s the fabric of the theatre had deteriorated. The theatre closed in 1889 for alterations and improvements, including a new entrance, dressing rooms and seating. Four shops were also added at the southern end, facing Regent Road. The last performance, *Aladdin*, finished in January 1929. The theatre closed and remained empty for five years until demolished in 1933 to make way for a new cinema, the Regal.

THE PILLAR BOX is still outside British Home Stores. The Theatre Royal was demolished and the Regal cinema/theatre was built on the site by J. Balls & Son of Northgate Street at a cost of £50,000. It opened on 1 January 1934 with the film *The Private Life of Henry VIII*, starring Charles Laughton. The first stage production was the pantomime *Mother Hubbard*. Yarmouth Amateur Operatic Society staged a musical comedy, the first of many here. My wife Susanne performed on this stage in many productions with this society. A lofty auditorium, with an unusually steep circle, accommodated 1,500 seats. The organ rose from the orchestra pit. In 1963 the Regal was renamed the ABC, and in 1987 it became the Cannon. Finally, sadly, in 1989, Yarmouth lost a fine building. After well over 200 years on this site, the building was demolished. Today we find shops here.

DENE SIDE METHODIST CHURCH

THE CHURCH WAS on the corner of Regent Road and Deneside. During the 1830s the trustees reported that the previous chapel, on the corner of King Street and Regent Road, was 'very dilapidated'. In the search for new premises a nearby builders' store was found. This site was bought, along with some adjacent shops and land along Deneside. Building work began in 1837; the opening service took place on 14 June 1838. The church originally had a south-facing main entrance on to Deneside, opening on to land known as 'Chapel Yard', to

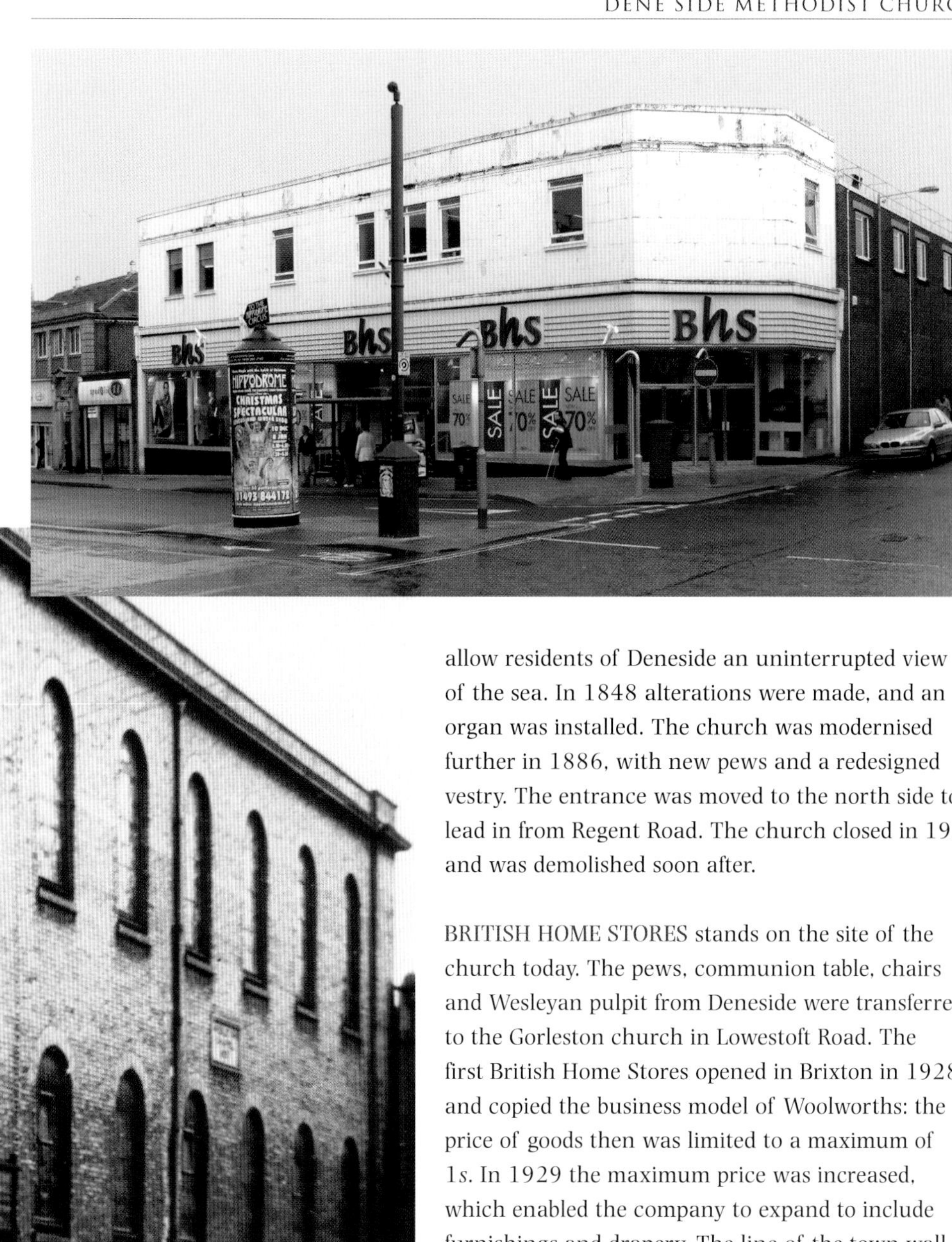

allow residents of Deneside an uninterrupted view of the sea. In 1848 alterations were made, and an organ was installed. The church was modernised further in 1886, with new pews and a redesigned vestry. The entrance was moved to the north side to lead in from Regent Road. The church closed in 1937 and was demolished soon after.

BRITISH HOME STORES stands on the site of the church today. The pews, communion table, chairs and Wesleyan pulpit from Deneside were transferred to the Gorleston church in Lowestoft Road. The first British Home Stores opened in Brixton in 1928 and copied the business model of Woolworths: the price of goods then was limited to a maximum of 1*s*. In 1929 the maximum price was increased, which enabled the company to expand to include furnishings and drapery. The line of the town wall runs between British Home Stores and 'Spud u like' on the east side of the store.

Great Yarmouth possesses one of the most complete medieval town walls in England. About two thirds of its original 2,236 yards survive, with eleven of the original eighteen towers. The building of the defences began in 1285; it was probably not finally finished before about 1400.

WOOLWORTHS, REGENT ROAD

A BUSY SUMMER'S day in Regent Road in the late 1950s. Woolworths, an American company established in 1879, opened their first UK store in Liverpool in 1909, selling children's clothing, stationary and toys, with a performance by a full orchestra, circus acts and fireworks. Woolworths took off in the mid-1920s, with stores opening as often as every three weeks. Work started building the Yarmouth Woolworths' store and the Dene Billiard Hall (advertising sixteen tables) in 1923, opening in 1925. Woolworths sold a large number of lines, and even by the late 1930s were still selling 'nothing over *6d*'. Woolworths closed the Regent Road store in 1959 and moved to their newly built store in the Market Place. Between Woolworths and Hilton's shoe shop is Currys – who are advertising televisions, then new to the town. BBC1 arrived in 1955, and ITV in 1959.

WOOLWORTHS HAS NOW gone but the building has survived. Fine Fare, the first national supermarket to come to the town, opened in the old Woolworths' store in 1962. McDonald's opened in 1985, with Lloyds Chemist and Kentucky Fried Chicken standing on the site today. Currys moved to the Market Place in 1978, the site now being 'Spud u like'. Hilton's shoe shop (to the right of the 1950s photograph) was in recent years absorbed by British Home Stores. Between Spud u like and British Home Stores, the fractured end of the town wall (now carefully smoothed) is seen. Straddling Regent Road at this point was a gate in the town wall, leading to a gap 21ft wide. Once named Oxney's – and in 1643, Steele's Gate, after families of that name – it was demolished in 1776. There were two principal gates, the north and south, with several smaller intermediate gates along the east wall.

ALEXANDRA ROAD

ALEXANDRA ROAD, LOOKING north. The west side was formerly ground belonging to Thomas Lettis. This was used as a ropemaker's spinning ground. The town council in 1857 purchased the ropewalk for £550; three houses were built on the site. St George's Gatehouse to the left is where Dr Vores resided in the 1870s. Later, Dr Wrigley lived in these premises. After his death in 1918 his wife continued to live here until it was demolished in 1936. The Nurses' Home was built on the site. Next door, at Calthorpe House, lived Charles Woolverton, mayor in 1868 and 1872. In the 1930s, Dr Smellie moved from King Street to these premises. Later the Stuart family resided here

until in 1972, when the Hospital Authority purchased the property. In the background Regent Road can be seen and Dene House, which stood on the corner of Regent Road and Alexandra Road.

ALEXANDRA ROAD TODAY is the main route for traffic through the town. The former Nurses' Home to the left, opened in 1937, cost £12,250 to build, with the furnishings adding another £4,000. Bedrooms for forty-two nurses were on the first and second floors. A night porter escorted the nurses back to the home after finishing night duty. Nurses had to be home by nine o'clock in the evening, unless they had been granted a late pass until half past ten. After the opening of the James Paget Hospital, the Nurses' Home closed and lay derelict for a few years. It was converted into one- and two-bedroom apartments in 2002. Calthorpe House has hardly changed over the years, but sadly today this fine building stands empty. The houses in Regent Road (seen in the earlier photograph) were all demolished to build the Market Place relief road, which opened in 1982.

ST GEORGE'S PARK

ST GEORGE'S PARK was laid out by the Corporation in 1866. It cost £449, and was constructed principally through the exertions of Edward Stagg, listed in a directory for 1869 as an auctioneer and estate agent. New tennis courts opened in 1886, and war memorials were added in 1922 and 1949, with the main column holding the details of the First World War's casualties, while a series of plaques commemorate the fallen of the Second. On the east side of the park (to the right of the image) was the large house and grounds of Isaac Preston. James Last's windmill, clearly visible over the buildings in Crown Road, stood north of Albion Road, next to the old

Catholic school. Today, modern town housing and a car park stand on the site. Note the fences: this was to keep in the sheep which were allowed to graze in the park. The trees look very young, as do the gravel walkways.

ST GEORGE'S PARK still provides a peaceful haven from the hustle and bustle of the town centre, only a few minutes' walk away. The park was built on the Dene's, where (until comparatively recent times) no buildings were allowed. These provided magnificent grazing for the livestock of rich and poor alike. In 2008, the park underwent a £2 million-plus refurbishment scheme which included improved lighting, security, new play equipment, seating, new pathways and planting of some new trees. Three entrance features were created by Norfolk blacksmiths. The herring arch, of ropes intertwined with herrings, seaweed and starfish, is situated at the town centre entrance. The second entrance, opposite St George's Chapel, depicts mooring chains, with seagulls perched aloft, while a third arch is of fishing nets and seaweed.

YARMOUTH GENERAL HOSPITAL

THE HOSPITAL WAS opened in 1840 at a cost of £1,600. It was built on a portion of the town wall and the Chapel Mount to the east of St George's Chapel. A boatman's lookout, built in 1774, had to be demolished. As compensation for this, a new lookout tower was built for the fishermen. This can be seen in the background. However, from this vantage point the men could look straight into the wards – so the windows were modified to prevent this. Later the lookout fell into disuse and was annexed to the hospital. In 1855 a new wing to the south was added for thirty inpatients; it can be

seen jutting out slightly from the building line. Plans for a further wing to the north were made, but never materialized. A new hospital was built on the site in 1887 to celebrate Queen Victoria's Jubilee.

THE HOSPITAL CLOSED in 1981 and was demolished a few years later. A time capsule, which had been placed under the foundation stone in 1887, was discovered containing a copy of the *Eastern Daily Press* for 18 May 1887, along with the annual report for 1886, a programme for the laying of the foundation stone and some coins. The capsule was opened live on BBC1 programme, *Look East*. Both hospitals were built on the Mount, the first substantial modification to the town walls. Work began in 1569 on a huge mound of earth which appeared to have had ten guns mounted in three tiers. Further work was carried out in 1587 due to rumours of the impending Spanish Armada. Remains of the East Mount were discovered in 1986 during demolition. Today St George's Court, residential housing, stands on the site.

KITTY WITCHES ROW

PROBABLY THE ROW that excites more curiosity than all the remaining ones is Row 95, Kitty Witches Row, which ran from King Street to Middlegate Street. It is extremely narrow at the west end – only 27in. A lady who lived in the Row stated 'if she pushed her pram in at the King Street end she could not get it out into Middlegate Street.' Before the Rows were illuminated this passageway was usually avoided by children at night: this Row bends considerably towards the south, while the lofty walls on either side gave it a gloomy appearance even on the brightest day, so rendering it a fit scene for mystery and darkness.

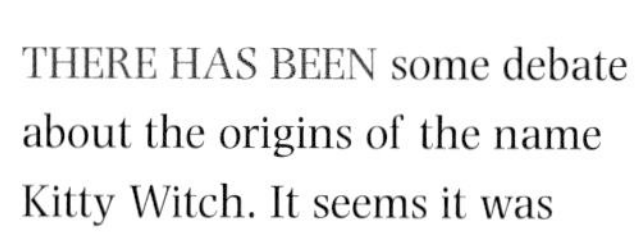

THERE HAS BEEN some debate about the origins of the name Kitty Witch. It seems it was customary many years ago at Yarmouth for women of the lowest order to go, in troops, from house to house. At each they would levy contributions. For some reason, one that no one seems to remember, the women wore men's shirts over their own apparel and their faces were smeared with blood. Perhaps this ceremony recalls a medieval (or even older) attack on the town, a time when the women, in the absence of the men, could have stood guard on the town walls – or even fought off invaders? The wearing of men's shirts might have been a tactic to deceive the enemy. It has also been suggested that the name is a corruption of a local's name.

THE TOLHOUSE

THE TOLHOUSE IS the oldest civic building in Britain. It was built as a private house for a rich merchant whose livelihood depended on the nearby quayside. The external stairway to the main hall can still be seen. By the thirteenth century it was in public use: the borough courts were held here, with the basement housing the town gaol, home of the notorious dungeon known as 'the hold' (note the hold window to the right of the stairway). The Tolhouse was restored in 1886 and later converted into a museum and library. To the right is Row 106. Next along is John Cutforth's chemist shop. To the left, on the corner of Row 108, is Wilson's shop: children spent their occasional coppers on aniseed balls at around forty for a penny; liquorice ladders were four for a penny. Dolly mixture and such like confectionery could also be purchased. The shop finally closed in 1974.

TOLHOUSE STREET TODAY, showing the Tolhouse, now a museum, restored after fire damage from two severe raids during the last war. The building seems almost out of place, a relic of a bygone age amongst modern houses. Wilson's old shop, the only shop in Middlegate Street to survive, is now used as a private house. The original front has changed little over the years. The library, also destroyed during the same air raid as damaged the Tolhouse in 1941, was rebuilt in 1959; the buildings between the Tolhouse and the Salvation Army Citadel were demolished to make the entrance for the new library. The Salvation Army Citadel was built as a hall and lodge rooms for the Friendly Societies in 1889.

MIDDLEGATE STREET

MIDDLEGATE STREET, *c.* 1943. Tolhouse Tavern public house is just visible on the left. The street was once called 'the street of all pubs': there was said to be one on almost every corner of the Rows. The Scottish fishermen had an outsize capacity for alcohol, but also had a liking for Yarmouth milk, crowding into the small shops in the street to drink numerous pints. Next along is Henry Culley, general shopkeeper, who 'patted up' butter and margarine and weighed out sugar in its traditional blue bags. Soda for the Monday wash was bagged up in the same way. Next along is Mr Newton's draper's, empty and damaged after bombing. Following on from Row 109, the shop to the far right was being run by Mrs Palmer in 1938. The sunlight on the door of the Tolhouse Tavern, behind the lamp post, is shining down from Row 108 opposite.

TOLHOUSE STREET, ONE of the three main streets that curved north to south in medieval times, was known as 'Great Middlegate'. It was later known as Gaol Street, and reverted back to Middlegate Street in 1870. The gaol in the Tolhouse opposite closed in 1875. To the left is Yarmouth Way, one of the new roads running east to west constructed in 1956. Docwras' sweet factory and Johnson's clothing manufactures were both demolished in 1954 to make way for this much-needed road. Middlegate Street from Yarmouth Way to Nottingham Way (another new roadway in 1952) was renamed Tolhouse Street, and the stretch from Hall Plain to Yarmouth Way was renamed Greyfriars Way. Redevelopment of Middlegate started in 1952. The keys for the first four tenants were handed over in November 1952.

TEA
LYONS TEA
Weights
GOLD FLAKE
OXO
LYONS TEA

HARRY CLARKE

MIDDLEGATE STREET, 1943. The tall building to the left is No. 41; next door is Jary's butcher's. Miss Dyball's draper's is next.

Mr Clarke (whose memories of Middlegate Street are found in this book) was born over this shop in 1932. A wall with a row of small windows separated his living quarters from Henry Davis's shop next door. This was the famous barber of Middlegate Street. Harry, as he was known, had a parrot which could swear better than most sailors. If Harry nipped to the pub for a quick drink and a customer showed up, the parrot would say 'he's in the pub'. Harry was one of many characters found in the street. The west end of Row 120 and the bombed shop of tailor Herbert Moore are next, with the end of Row 121 to the far right.

TOLHOUSE STREET TODAY, looking towards the rear of the premises on the west side of King Street. The ends of the Rows still survive today in the principal streets of the old town. The end of Row 121 is in the far background, just to the left of the tree. The street was devastated in 1941. One bomb on the 8 April wrecked more houses in a few seconds than scores of demolition men could have done in months of intensive work. Other raids during that year added to the work of demolition. Later in the war, part of the area was used as a battle school for soldiers training for house-to-house fighting. Thus by the end of the war not many of the buildings were worth preserving, becoming one of the several reconstruction areas in the town.

STORES

49-52 MIDDLEGATE STREET

MIDDLEGATE STREET IN 1946, just after the war, showing that perhaps part of the street could have been saved: these buildings, although damaged, do not look beyond repair. Row 125 is to the far left. It was known as 'Gun Row' after a gun barrel which was used as a post to stop carts damaging the corners of the buildings.

Follow on to No. 49, home to Thomas Brown, a grocer. It was usual for these shops to open from 6 a.m. to 10 p.m. Bircham and Stringer, a well-known butcher's, was next door. As this image shows, all the windows had been blown out during the war. Goulder's, the cycle shop with the sign above the entrance to Row 127, was at No. 51. In the 1930s the Goulder family ran a baker's shop here, which sold dumplings for 1*d*, or would cook your Sunday dinner for 2*d*. On most Sundays a queue would form outside the shop to cook dinners in the baker's ovens.

THE EAST SIDE of Tolhouse Street. The planning and progress of rebuilding was slow, partly because of the great number of individual owners involved. The first phase consisted of ninety-two dwellings laid out between Middlegate Street and King Street, facing Friars Lane. Work began in June 1952, initially on a block of three-bedroom houses. After the complete reconstruction work had been carried out, over 500 dwellings had been built on a site of about 20 acres. Vast areas of the unique Rows were destroyed by enemy action: so much of the history of the town was in these Rows, and the town can never be the same without them.

WELDING
&
BRAZING
CYCLE REPAIRS A SPECIALITY
CYCLE
ENGINEER.

ST PETER'S PAVED ROW EAST

ST PETER'S ROW, Row 130, ran from King Street to Middlegate Street. This Row was one of the first to be paved. Carts were not allowed to enter. Pedestrians preferred these pathways to the pebbly surfaces of the unpaved Rows, and so they became the locality of choice for shopkeepers. In 1905 seven shops were trading in this Row. This was an unusual feature, as hardly any shops existed in the other Rows. Broad Row and Market Row were the two exceptions, as these were also paved.

The Old White Lion public house can just be seen on the left. It had been a tavern for at least two and half centuries, and before that it was the house of a wealthy merchant. On the other corner of the Row is the fruit shop belonging to Mr Hover. Leach's ironmongers (Market Place) purchased these premises in around 1875. It was an essential resource, needed to cope with the increasing demands of the fishing trade, but finally closed here in the late 1920s.

NOTTINGHAM WAY, CONSTRUCTED in 1952. The southern pavement follows the line of the old Row 130. Two original shops listed in a directory for 1923 – Mrs Smith's, a wardrobe dealer at No. 22, and the premises of Arthur Storey, a bootmaker, at No. 23 – survived the demolition. Today Nos 60-62 Nottingham Way comprise of a computer shop and a private house. Unfortunately the gradual elimination of private traders, with their quaint shop fronts, proved to be one of the penalties of progress. To our grandfathers and fathers the Rows and back streets were important places, associated for many generations with cabinet-makers, clock-makers, bakers and many other trades. The shops opened at all hours, and even at midnight the old trader would have been reluctant to close his books. In streets like Middlegate, many of these shops were found on the corners of the Rows. The Old White Lion is still on the corner, though sadly it is no longer a public house.

FRUITERER

ST PETER'S PAVED ROW WEST

ROW 129 IS another paved Row running from Middlegate Street to South Quay. This, with Row 130, was once a main thoroughfare from the Quay to King Street. The shop with clothing hanging outside was a tailor's shop run by Mr Clare. In 1905 Porritt and Currey, a pawnbroker's, traded here. What tales of hardship lay within this shop? The Row of terraced houses with the railings in front has been built back from the road, an early attempt to widen the Row to let more light into the otherwise gloomy rooms. Shutters can be seen on the windows, a feature added to the houses to improve privacy. Is the lady with the jug on her way to the pub, or to the shop to buy milk for the children? A lamp lights the Row. Walking through the Rows at night during the last war – with the blackout in place – was not for the faint-hearted!

NOTTINGHAM WAY TODAY is a main route across the town. The line of Row 129 is just to the right of the pavement on the south side. Locals call the complete estate, from Yarmouth Way to Friars Lane, Middlegate. When the first tenants moved in it was described as 'a neighbourhood of brand new well-planned labour saving flats, maisonettes and houses built in the reconstruction area; a site which for over ten years had been left derelict.'

By the late 1980s the council approved a massive £7.5 million improvement scheme for the estate over at least ten years. Lack of privacy and security led to problems, with pavements and walkways strewn with rubbish. Many walls were covered in graffiti; rooms echoed with the constant sound of running water from countless overflow pipes; gardens were overgrown. The plan was to divide the estate up into communities of about fifty houses each. This photograph shows these improvements.

KING STREET

KING STREET IN 1947, looking north. Row 135 and a half is to the left, a half Row which ran to the rear of the Cock Tavern, a public house in Middlegate Street later renamed the Middlegate Tavern. Next along is the British Legion Club, the fine building with the flagpole outside on the corner of the Row. This was established in 1919. The other corner of the Row, just visible, was Blanchflower's potted meat and game factory. The business had been sold to the Co-op by 1923 and became the Co-op Canning Factory. Note the lamp post, still with its

war-time white lines. The buildings all look damaged, but not beyond repair. Sadly, however, all of this line as far as the tall, bay-fronted building in the far background – including Rows 131, 134 and 135 – was demolished. The bus is about to turn into St Peter's Road.

KING STREET TODAY. Before the war, this part of Yarmouth was where density of houses was at its highest – and the amenities obtainable in them at their lowest. A great part of the area had been scheduled before the war for clearance as a slum, but nothing was done when the outbreak of hostilities put an end to hopes of any improvements. This area was phase one of the reconstruction areas in 1952, with the average cost of a dwelling £1,500. When the complete estate was finished some 500 dwellings had been built. Mrs Jarrod, one of the first tenants, compared the well-lighted rooms and pretty colour schemes with the old rooms in which she used to live, behind a shop in Middlegate Street, where it was so dark that they had to have the light on from six in the morning to eleven at night.

FRIAR'S LANE

FRIAR'S LANE RAN from South Quay to Deneside. The photograph shows the buildings at the east end looking on to the south side of the road. The buildings with the slope in front were all built up against the town wall. The Blackfriars were established in this part of the town by 1260. In some documents the road was known as 'South Street', this being the original east-west road at this end of the town. At the bottom of the slope in the photograph, just to the left of the house that stands proud, was a passageway named 'Adam and Eve Passage'. Large gardens and orchards are known to have existed in the grounds of the Blackfriars. Did the orchard have some

bearing on the name of the passage? By the early part of the nineteenth century the Blackfriars' site had been completely built over.

FRIARS LANE TODAY. The buildings shown in the old photograph have been demolished, exposing the town wall. Adam and Eve passageway is still a walkway but no remains whatsoever mark the site of the monastery. When the new fire station was built in 1971 on part of the friar's enclosure some remains of the church, which ran from east to west, were found. The church was also thought to extend underneath the Clipper Schooner public house shown in the background. The church could have been as long as St Nicholas' church.

Several skeletons were found some 3ft below the level of the church floor. A stone coffin was found close to the north wall of the church. It did not have a lid, and contained the remains of a human skeleton. I was given permission to be on site during the build, and witnessed this find myself.

BENNETT'S STORES, 111 KING STREET

THIS PHOTOGRAPH SHOWS Bennett's grocery shop with all the staff posing outside, while a small child looks on from the upstairs window. Mr Bennett also had a shop on the corner of Churchill Road. The assistants there would cut the amount of cheese required with a steel wire and neatly wrap it. The bacon slicer had a big handle and a sound of its own as it cut the large joints of ham and meat. This shop, like the Maypole, Home and Colonial and similar

shops, had a smell and atmosphere that could never be reproduced in the modern supermarket of today. Note the number of staff and of course the prices in the windows. The young whistling errand boy would deliver your orders on a trade bike. The wartime grocer carefully wrapped the butter to ensure that the customer only received the ration of 2oz a week.

STAR SUPPLY STORES was trading here by 1927. In the late 1960s the name was changed to the International Stores. Only if a supermarket has a delicatessen counter are you today able to find some sort of personal service. A pretend shop with small tins and cash register was once a gift; I have never seen our granddaughters playing at grocery shops. A cardboard box once seemed to accommodate everything; you cannot help but wonder why nowadays the average family seems to require a supermarket trolley laden with umpteen bags. The cashier in the old grocer shops sat at a desk in a cubicle; today, lines of tills are found in supermarkets. In years to come these will vanish, to be replaced by automatic tills. Sadly, Bennett's old shop has been demolished; it was turned into a beer garden for the Old White Lion next door, which today stands forgotten and empty.

If you enjoyed this book, you may also be interested in…

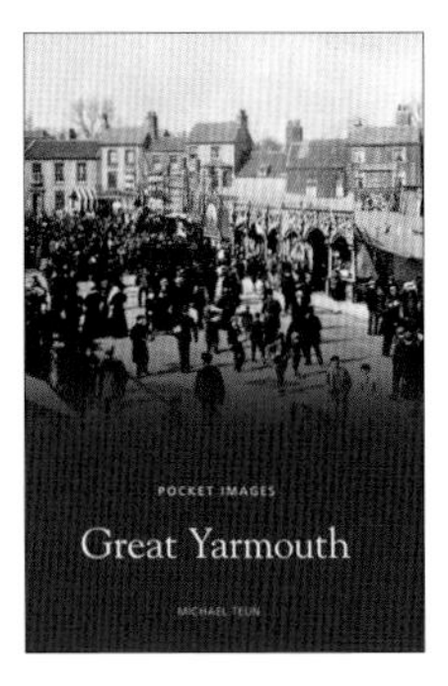

Great Yarmouth

MIICHAEL TEUN

Since the Middle Ages, the lives of kings, vagabonds, artists, authors, poets and peasants – Lord Nelson, Charles Dickens, Sir James Paget and Lady Hamilton, to name but a few – have all been part of Great Yarmouth. The rich history of this port and resort at the mouth of the River Yare is reflected in this selection of over 200 photographs from the collection of local history enthusiast Michael Teun. This book will evoke nostalgic memories for many.

978 1 8458 8418 5

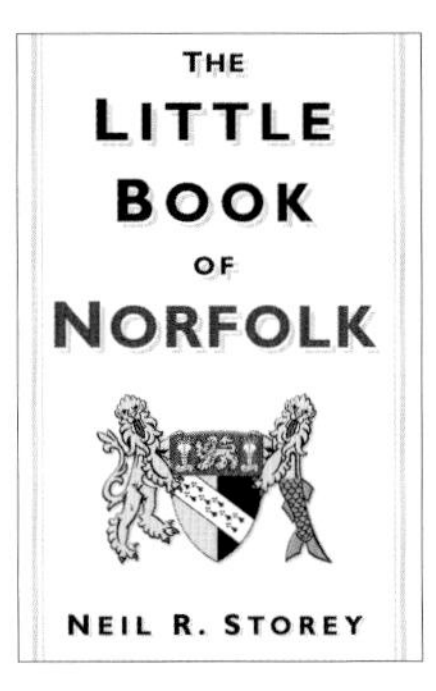

The Little Book of Norfolk

NEIL R. STOREY

Here is a repository of intriguing, fascinating, obscure, strange and entertaining facts and trivia about one of England's most colourful counties. It is an essential to the born and bred Norfolk folk or anyone who knows and loves the county. Armed with this fascinating tome the reader will have such knowledge of the county, its landscape, people, places, pleasures and pursuits they will be entertained and enthralled and never short of some frivolous fact to enhance conversation or quiz!

978 0 7524 6160 1

Country Boy: Growing up in Norfolk 1940-60

COLIN MILLER

Colin Miller was born in 1940 in Rollesby, a village in the heart of Broadland Norfolk. In Rollesby, as in so many other rural communities at this time, drinking water was from a well, the lavatory was a bucket in an outside privy, transport was a bicycle or a bus and entertainment was provided by the radio, whist drives at the village hall or a rare visit to the cinema. It will bring back many memories for anyone who grew up in rural Britain in the 1940s and '50s.

978 0 7509 4247 8

A Grim Almanac of Norfolk

NEIL R. STOREY

Like to know more about the darker side of Norfolk's history? If so, enquire within! This almanac explores dreadful deeds, macabre deaths, strange occurrences and grim tales from the shadier side of the county's past. Jostling for position in this cornucopia of the criminal and curious are diverse tales of highwaymen, smugglers, murderers, bodysnatchers, duellists, footpads, poachers, rioters and rebels, bizarre funerals, disasters and peculiar medicine. If it's horrible, if it's ghastly, if it's strange, it's here!

978 0 7524 5680 5

Visit our website and discover thousands of other History Press books.

www.thehistorypress.co.uk